Colorado Bingo Book

COMPLETE BINGO GAME IN A BOOK

Written By Rebecca Stark
Educational Books 'n' Bingo

TITLE: Colorado Bingo
AUTHOR: Rebecca Stark

ISBN 978-0-87386-499-2

Educational Books 'n' Bingo

Printed in the U.S.A.

DIRECTIONS

1. **Either cut apart the book or make copies of ALL the sheets. You might want to make an extra copy of the clue sheets to use for introduction and review. Keep the sheets in an envelope for easy reuse.**

2. Cut apart the call sheets with terms and clues.

3. Pass out one bingo sheet per student. There are enough unique sheets for a class of 30.

4. Pass out the markers. You may cut apart the markers included in this book or use any other small items of your choice. Students can also mark the sheets themselves; recopy the sheets as needed for additional games.

5. Decide whether or not you will require the entire sheet to be filled. Requiring the entire sheet to be filled provides a better review. However, if you have a short time to fill, you may prefer to have them do the just the border or some other format. Tell the class before you begin what is required.

6. There are 50 terms. Read the list before you begin. If there are any terms that have not been covered in class, you may want to read to the students the term and clues before you begin.

7. There is a blank space in the middle of each sheet. You can instruct the students to use it as a free space or you can write in answers to cover terms not included. Of course, in this case you would create your own clues. (Templates provided.)

8. Shuffle the sheets and place them in a pile. Two or three clues are provided for each term. If you plan to play the game with the same group more than once, you might want to choose a different clue for each game. If not, you may choose to use more than one clue.

9. Be sure to keep the sheets you have used for the present game in a separate pile. When a student calls, "Bingo," he or she will have to verify that the correct answers are on his or her sheet AND that the markers were placed in response to the proper questions. Pull out the sheets that are on the student's sheet keeping them in the order they were used in the game. Read each clue as it was given and ask the student to identify the correct answer from his or her sheet.

10. If the student has the correct answers on the sheet AND has shown that they were marked in response to the *correct questions,* then that student is the winner and the game is over. If the student does not have the correct answers on the sheet OR he or she marked the answers in response to *the wrong questions,* then the game continues until there is a proper winner.

11. If you want to play again, reshuffle the sheets and begin again.

Have fun

TERMS INCLUDED

Aquamarine

Aurora

Basin

Bighorn Sheep

Blue Spruce

Border (-ed)

Boulder

Canyon

Centennial State

Climate

Coloradan(s)

Colorado Hairstreak

Colorado River

Colorado Springs

Colorado Territory

Colorado War

Columbine

Continental Divide

County (-ies)

Crop(s)

Denver

Executive Branch

Flag

Four Corners

Georgetown Loop Railroad

Gold

Grand Junction

Great Plains

Highest

Judicial Branch

Lake(s)

Lark Bunting

Legislative Branch

Livestock

Louisiana Purchase

Mesa

Mining (-ed)

Motto

National Park(s)

Painted Turtle

Pikes Peak

Plateau

Rhodochrosite

Rivers

Rocky Mountain(s)

Ski (-ing)

Song(s)

Stegosaurus

Tiger Salamander

Wings Over the Rockies

Additional Terms

Choose as many additional terms as you would like and write them in the squares. Repeat each as desired.
Cut out the squares and randomly distribute them to the class.
Instruct the students to place their square on the center space of their card.

Colorado Bingo

Clues for Additional Terms

Write three clues for each of your additional terms.

_____ 1. 2. 3.	_____ 1. 2. 3.
_____ 1. 2. 3.	_____ 1. 2. 3.
_____ 1. 2. 3.	_____ 1. 2. 3.

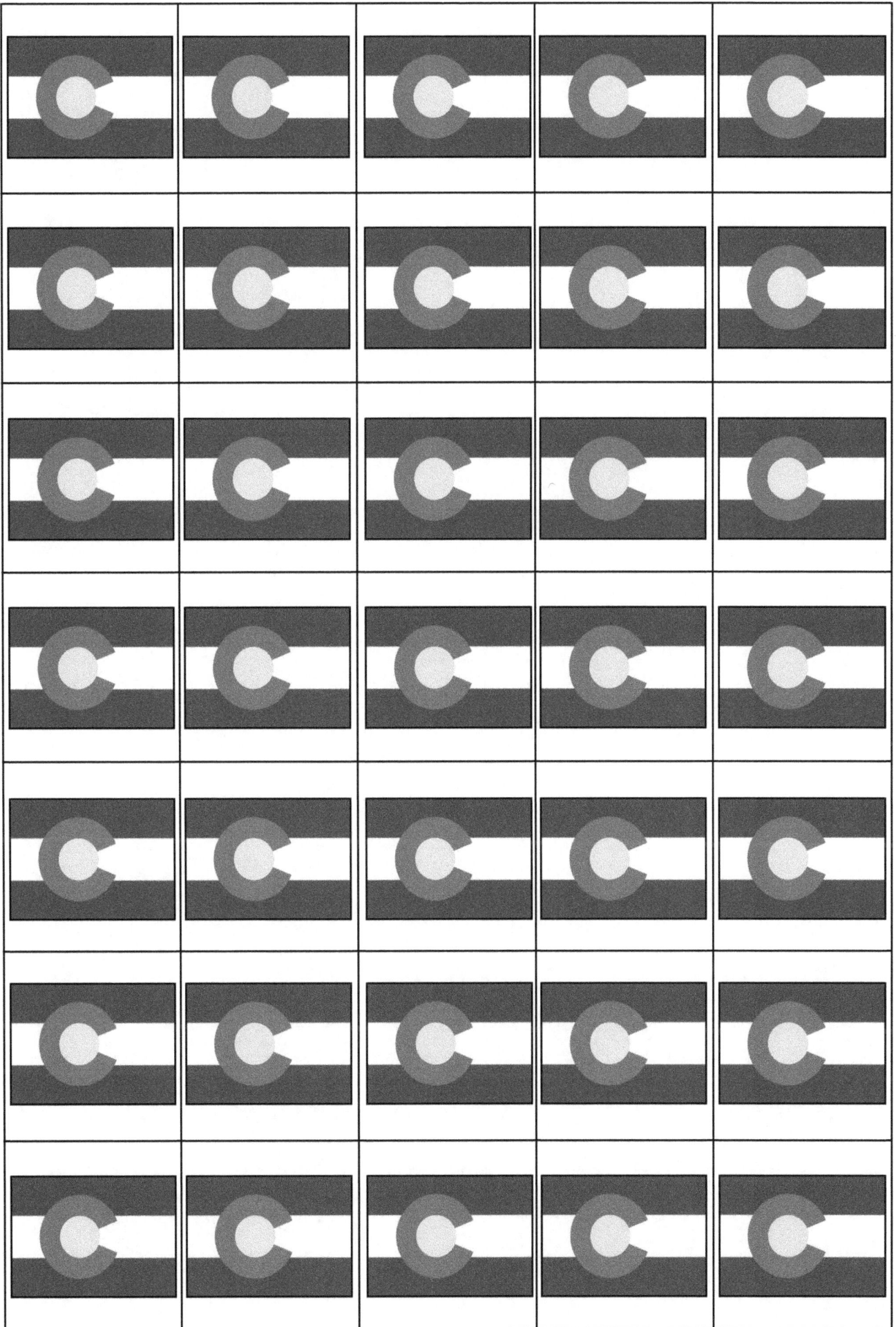

Aquamarine
1. The ___ is the state gem. It is a member of the beryl family. Crystals range in color from shades of green-blue to blue.
2. Quality gem ___ crystals can be found in the mountain peaks of Mount Antero and White Mountain.

Aurora
1. ___ is the third largest city after Denver and Colorado Springs.
2. ___ and Denver are the main cities in the Denver Metropolitan Area. Buckley Air Force Base is in ___.

Basin
1. The Intermontane, or Intermountain, ___ is the smallest land area of Colorado. It covers the northwest corner of the state.
2. This small land area of Colorado is characterized by rolling forested hills, plateaus and sagebrush.

Bighorn Sheep
1. The Rocky Mountain ___ is the state mammal.
2. This mammal can be found above the timberline in the rugged mountainous areas of the state.

Blue Spruce
1. The Colorado ___ is the state tree.
2. This tree is known for its majestic, symmetrical form and its beautiful silver-blue color.

Border (-ed)
1. Colorado is ___ by Wyoming, Nebraska, New Mexico, Oklahoma, Kansas, and Utah.
2. Colorado is one of only three states with no natural ___, the others being Wyoming and Utah.

Boulder
1. The main campus of the University of Colorado is located in ___.
2. The Flatirons are rock formations near ___. They have become a symbol of that city.

Canyon
1. Black ___ of the Gunnison is a national park. It was sculpted by the Gunnison River.
2. A ___ is a deep ravine between cliffs, often carved from the landscape by a river.

Centennial State
1. Colorado is nicknamed the ___ because it entered the Union in 1876.
2. This nickname refers to the fact that Colorado became a state 100 years after the signing of the *Declaration of Independence.*

Climate
1. The ___ of Colorado is semi-arid. Precipitation gradually increases as you go eastward.
2. The combination of high elevation and middle latitude generally results in a cool, dry ___. Local areas differ because of differences in elevation.

Colorado Bingo

Coloradan(s) 1. This is what a person from Colorado is called. 2. At one time ___ were nicknamed Silverines because of the rich silver mines in the state.	**Colorado Hairstreak** 1. The ___ butterfly is the state insect. 2. The upper side of the ___'s wings are purple with a dark border.
Colorado River 1. The ___ is the most important river in the southwestern United States. It gets its name from the reddish silt it carries from the mountains. 2. The ___ rises in the Rocky Mountains and flows across the Colorado Plateau.	**Colorado Springs** 1. The U.S. Air Force Academy is in ___. 2. ___ sits at the foot of Pike's Peak. It is the second most populous city in the state.
Colorado Territory 1. Soon after the Pike's Peak Gold Rush of 1858 to 1861, the region around Pikes Peak was organized as ___. 2. ___ existed from February 28, 1861, until August 1, 1876, when Colorado became the 38th state.	**Colorado War** 1. In the ___ the Cheyenne and Arapaho tribes fought against white settlers and the militia in the Colorado Territory. 2. The ___ was fought from 1863 to 1865. It was fought over control of the bison migration grounds.
Columbine 1. The white and lavender ___ is the state flower. 2. In 1925 the Colorado General Assembly approved a bill that made it the responsibility of all Coloradans to protect the white and lavender ___.	**Continental Divide** 1. The ___ is the dividing line separating river systems that flow to opposite sides of a continent. 2. On the eastern side of the ___ all rivers and streams flow towards the Gulf of Mexico and the Atlantic Ocean. On the western side all water flows towards the Pacific Ocean.
County (-ies) 1. Colorado is divided into 64 governing districts called ___. 2. Two of the 64 ___ have consolidated city and ___ governments. They are Denver and Broomfield. Colorado Bingo	**Crop(s)** 1. Important field ___ are wheat, corn and hay. Beans, grain sorghum, potatoes and sugar beets are also produced. 2. Apples are the leading fruit ___. © Barbara M. Peller

Denver
1. It is the capital and the largest city in Colorado.
2. ___ is nicknamed The Mile-High City.

Executive Branch
1. The ___ comprises the governor, the lieutenant governor, the secretary of state, the state treasurer, and the attorney general.
2. The governor is head of the ___; the present-day governor is [fill in].

Flag
1. There are three alternate stripes on the state ___, two blue and one white.
2. The color of the "C" on the state ___ is red. Its center is filled with the color gold to represent the state's abundant sunshine.

Four Corners
1. Colorado, New Mexico, Arizona, and Utah meet at one common point known as the ___.
2. Colorado is not bordered by Arizona, but it meets it at its southwest corner. This spot is known as the ___.

Georgetown Loop Railroad
1. This stretch of narrow-gauge railroad was completed in 1884 and was an engineering marvel for its time.
2. The ___ connected the thriving mining towns of Georgetown and Silver Plume during the silver boom of the 1880s.

Gold
1. Participants in the ___ rush were known as "fifty-niners" after 1859, the peak year of the rush. Their motto was "Pike's Peak or Bust!"
2. The discovery of ___ led to the migration of around 50,000 people to Colorado between 1858 and 1859.

Grand Junction
1. This city is located along the Colorado River, where it meets the Gunnison River.
2. ___ has been given the nickname "River City."

Great Plains
1. The ___ is a large grassland prairie ecosystem that extends from Northern Canada to Southern Texas and east from the Rocky Mountains.
2. Much of the eastern half of Colorado is part of this grassland prairie ecosystem.

Highest
1. Colorado is sometimes called the ___ state because it has a higher mean elevation than any other state.
2. Mt. Elbert at 14,433 feet is the ___ point in the state.

Judicial Branch
1. The ___ interprets what our laws mean and makes decisions about the laws and those who break them.
2. The ___ is made up of several courts, the highest of which is the state Supreme Court.

Colorado Bingo

Lake(s)	**Lark Bunting**
1. Colorado has more than 2,000 ___ and reservoirs. Grand ___, Blue Mesa Reservoir, and John Martin Reservoir are a few. 2. Grand ___ is the largest and deepest natural ___ in the state. Blue Mesa Reservoir is the largest reservoir when filled to capacity.	1. The ___ is the official bird of Colorado. 2. The ___ is a medium-sized sparrow.
Legislative Branch	**Livestock**
1. The ___ is responsible for making the laws in Colorado. 2. The General Assembly is the ___ of government; it comprises the House of Representatives and the Senate.	1. More than 60% of the state's agricultural revenues are from ___ and ___ products. 2. Cattle and calves are the main ___ products. Others include hogs, sheep, lambs, dairy products and chicken eggs.
Louisiana Purchase	**Mesa**
1. The eastern part of what was to become Colorado was included in the ___ of 1803. 2. The ___ was the largest land purchase in the history of the United States. It doubled the nation's size.	1. Grand ___ reaches heights of over 11,000 feet. It was formed by erosion caused by the flow of the Colorado and the Gunnison rivers. 2. A ___ is an elevated area of land with a flat top and steep sides. It gets its name from the Spanish word for "table."
Mining (-ed)	**Motto**
1. Colorado's ___ industry is important. Oil, coal, and natural gas are the most important ___ products. 2. Other important ___ products include sand and gravel, gold, and molybdenum.	1. The state ___ is the Latin phrase *"Nil Sine Numine."* The translation is "Nothing Without Providence" or "Nothing without the Deity." 2. The ___ of the fifty-niners was "Pike's Peak or Bust!"
National Park(s)	**Painted Turtle**
1. Rocky Mountain, Mesa Verde, Great Sand Dunes, and Black Canyon of the Gunnison are ___ in Colorado. 2. Rocky Mountain ___ is one of the most visited ___ in the nation. Its Trail Ridge Road crests over 12,000 feet.	1. The western ___ is the state reptile. 2. This reptile has a smooth, oval, top shell; olive skin; and red, orange, or yellow stripes on its extremities.

Colorado Bingo

Pikes Peak 1. Originally called "El Capitán" by Spanish settlers, this mountain was renamed in honor of the explorer who led an expedition to the southern Colorado area in 1806. 2. Colorado Springs sits at the foot of ___.	**Plateau** 1. The Colorado ___ region is west of the Rocky Mountains. It covers the western fifth of the state. 2. The Colorado ___ runs along the border of Utah. It is an area of hills, deep valleys, plateaus and mesas.
Rhodochrosite 1. ___ is the state mineral. 2. ___ is a manganese carbonate mineral; it is deep red to rose pink.	**Rivers** 1. Colorado is the headwaters for nearly two dozen major ___, including the Colorado, the Rio Grande, the Animas, and the Arkansas. 2. Because they are on the western side of the Continental Divide, Colorado's ___ flow towards the Pacific Ocean.
Rocky Mountain(s) 1. Front Range, Sangre de Cristo Mountains, Park Range, Sawatch Range and San Juan Mountains are all part of this major mountain range. 2. The ___ stretch more than 3,000 miles from British Columbia in western Canada to New Mexico.	**Ski (-ing)** 1. Vail and Aspen are popular ___ resorts in Colorado. 2. Many tourists come to Colorado for the ___ and snowboarding.
Song(s) 1. "Where the Columbines Grow" has been the state ___ since 1915. 2. In 2007 a second state ___ was added: "Rocky Mountain High."	**Stegosaurus** 1. ___ is the state fossil. Fossils of this dinosaur have been found in Morrison, Colorado. 2. This quadrupedal dinosaur had a double row of kite-shaped plates rising along its rounded back and two pairs of long spikes extending horizontally near the end of its tail.
Tiger Salamander 1. The state amphibian is the western ___. 2. Fossils of this amphibian were found in the Snowmass Village Ice Excavation.	**Wings Over the Rockies** 1. ___ is an Air and Space Museum. 2. This museum is located on the former grounds of Lowry Air Force Base in Denver, Colorado.

Colorado Bingo

Colorado Bingo

Motto	Aquamarine	Basin	County (-ies)	Blue Spruce
Columbine	Aurora	Stegosaurus	Judicial Branch	Pikes Peak
Song(s)	Highest		Louisiana Purchase	Tiger Salamander
Ski (-ing)	Painted Turtle	Rocky Mountain(s)	Great Plains	Lark Bunting
Livestock	Executive Branch	Colorado Springs	Rhodochrosite	Georgetown Loop Railroad

Colorado Bingo: Card No. 1

Colorado Bingo

Ski (-ing)	Song(s)	Four Corners	National Park(s)	Grand Junction
Lark Bunting	Colorado Territory	Canyon	Painted Turtle	Legislative Branch
Climate	Executive Branch		Flag	Rocky Mountain(s)
Mesa	Mining (-ed)	Highest	Wings Over the Rockies	Blue Spruce
Pikes Peak	Stegosaurus	Colorado Springs	Columbine	Rhodochrosite

Colorado Bingo: Card No. 2

Colorado Bingo

Executive Branch	Rocky Mountain(s)	Colorado Territory	Great Plains	Song(s)
Lark Bunting	Aurora	Centennial State	Aquamarine	Denver
Painted Turtle	Stegosaurus		Legislative Branch	Bighorn Sheep
Highest	Climate	Livestock	Mesa	Four Corners
Rhodochrosite	Coloradan(s)	Colorado Springs	Wings Over the Rockies	Grand Junction

Colorado Bingo: Card No. 3

Colorado Bingo

Highest	Legislative Branch	Basin	Coloradan(s)	Grand Junction
Lake(s)	Boulder	Aquamarine	National Park(s)	Song(s)
Louisiana Purchase	Mesa		Georgetown Loop Railroad	County (-ies)
Rocky Mountain(s)	Aurora	Stegosaurus	Colorado Springs	Canyon
Colorado Hairstreak	Pikes Peak	Border (-ed)	Rhodochrosite	Tiger Salamander

Colorado Bingo

Pikes Peak	Blue Spruce	Painted Turtle	Canyon	Coloradan(s)
Lake(s)	Rocky Mountain(s)	Centennial State	Flag	Aurora
Basin	Tiger Salamander		Judicial Branch	Crop(s)
Georgetown Loop Railroad	Grand Junction	Motto	Wings Over the Rockies	Colorado River
Colorado Territory	Colorado Springs	Song(s)	Highest	Louisiana Purchase

© Barbara M. Peller

Colorado Bingo

Bighorn Sheep	Legislative Branch	Four Corners	Grand Junction	Tiger Salamander
Great Plains	Painted Turtle	Colorado River	Aquamarine	Song(s)
National Park(s)	Colorado Hairstreak		Boulder	Flag
Colorado Springs	Livestock	Wings Over the Rockies	Border (-ed)	Basin
Lark Bunting	Canyon	Motto	Louisiana Purchase	Colorado War

Colorado Bingo

Motto	Legislative Branch	Crop(s)	Rocky Mountain(s)	Colorado Territory
Lark Bunting	Grand Junction	Executive Branch	Aurora	Lake(s)
Tiger Salamander	County (-ies)		Flag	Boulder
Highest	Mesa	Centennial State	Ski (-ing)	Climate
Colorado Springs	Coloradan(s)	Wings Over the Rockies	Border (-ed)	Bighorn Sheep

Colorado Bingo: Card No. 7

Colorado Bingo

Louisiana Purchase	Legislative Branch	Continental Divide	Great Plains	Boulder
Lake(s)	Basin	National Park(s)	Tiger Salamander	Canyon
Colorado War	Coloradan(s)		Grand Junction	Blue Spruce
Rhodochrosite	Highest	Ski (-ing)	Colorado Hairstreak	Mesa
Stegosaurus	Colorado Springs	Border (-ed)	Painted Turtle	Lark Bunting

Colorado Bingo: Card No. 8

Colorado Bingo

Flag	Colorado Territory	Executive Branch	Colorado War	Coloradan(s)
Colorado Hairstreak	Grand Junction	Louisiana Purchase	Painted Turtle	Legislative Branch
Denver	Motto		Aurora	Continental Divide
Colorado River	Blue Spruce	Livestock	Judicial Branch	Crop(s)
Mesa	Wings Over the Rockies	Centennial State	Ski (-ing)	Georgetown Loop Railroad

Colorado Bingo: Card No. 9

Colorado Bingo

Ski (-ing)	Great Plains	Boulder	National Park(s)	Colorado War
Tiger Salamander	Canyon	Aquamarine	Aurora	Grand Junction
Coloradan(s)	Legislative Branch		County (-ies)	Climate
Livestock	Georgetown Loop Railroad	Colorado River	Wings Over the Rockies	Denver
Centennial State	Lark Bunting	Four Corners	Pikes Peak	Louisiana Purchase

Colorado Bingo: Card No. 10

Colorado Bingo

Bighorn Sheep	Legislative Branch	Painted Turtle	Colorado River	Lark Bunting
Continental Divide	Denver	Judicial Branch	Flag	Aquamarine
Lake(s)	Grand Junction		Four Corners	Executive Branch
Centennial State	Song(s)	Wings Over the Rockies	Coloradan(s)	Ski (-ing)
Colorado Hairstreak	Colorado Springs	Motto	Border (-ed)	Colorado Territory

Colorado Bingo: Card No. 11

Colorado Bingo

Colorado Territory	Blue Spruce	Denver	Great Plains	Flag
Executive Branch	Lark Bunting	Basin	Border (-ed)	Aurora
Motto	Crop(s)		Tiger Salamander	National Park(s)
Colorado Springs	Mesa	Grand Junction	Ski (-ing)	Lake(s)
Legislative Branch	Continental Divide	Coloradan(s)	Colorado Hairstreak	Canyon

Colorado Bingo: Card No. 12

© Barbara M. Peller

Colorado Bingo

Colorado River	Blue Spruce	Bighorn Sheep	Denver	Tiger Salamander
Basin	Continental Divide	Grand Junction	Flag	Climate
Great Plains	Canyon		Executive Branch	Crop(s)
Louisiana Purchase	Wings Over the Rockies	Boulder	Coloradan(s)	Ski (-ing)
Colorado Springs	Georgetown Loop Railroad	Border (-ed)	Motto	Judicial Branch

Colorado Bingo: Card No. 13

Colorado Bingo

Columbine	Grand Junction	Painted Turtle	Flag	Colorado Hairstreak
Canyon	Motto	Denver	Aurora	Legislative Branch
Colorado River	County (-ies)		Four Corners	Centennial State
Georgetown Loop Railroad	Wings Over the Rockies	Coloradan(s)	Boulder	Bighorn Sheep
Colorado Springs	National Park(s)	Climate	Lark Bunting	Louisiana Purchase

Colorado Bingo: Card No. 14

Colorado Bingo

Judicial Branch	Flag	Painted Turtle	Colorado Territory	Great Plains
Bighorn Sheep	Four Corners	Aquamarine	Basin	Colorado Hairstreak
Tiger Salamander	Motto		Song(s)	Legislative Branch
Colorado Springs	Denver	Continental Divide	Wings Over the Rockies	Colorado River
Lark Bunting	Mesa	Border (-ed)	Colorado War	Executive Branch

Colorado Bingo

Boulder	Denver	Continental Divide	Colorado War	Mining (-ed)
National Park(s)	Climate	Crop(s)	Lake(s)	County (-ies)
Colorado River	Blue Spruce		Tiger Salamander	Executive Branch
Highest	Canyon	Colorado Springs	Judicial Branch	Ski (-ing)
Colorado Hairstreak	Rivers	Border (-ed)	Mesa	Legislative Branch

Colorado Bingo

Centennial State	Plateau	Gold	Denver	Columbine
Judicial Branch	Colorado Hairstreak	Wings Over the Rockies	County (-ies)	Crop(s)
Flag	Louisiana Purchase		Rivers	Continental Divide
Georgetown Loop Railroad	Lark Bunting	Ski (-ing)	Painted Turtle	Climate
Livestock	Colorado River	Colorado Territory	Great Plains	Blue Spruce

Colorado Bingo

Colorado War	Coloradan(s)	Canyon	Colorado River	National Park(s)
Legislative Branch	Centennial State	Livestock	Tiger Salamander	Colorado Hairstreak
Flag	Climate		Gold	Basin
Blue Spruce	Aquamarine	Wings Over the Rockies	Ski (-ing)	Four Corners
Rivers	Denver	Painted Turtle	Plateau	Bighorn Sheep

Colorado Bingo: Card No. 18

Colorado Bingo

Tiger Salamander	Bighorn Sheep	Denver	Continental Divide	Ski (-ing)
Judicial Branch	Great Plains	Legislative Branch	Colorado Territory	County (-ies)
Plateau	Coloradan(s)		Aurora	Song(s)
Four Corners	Rivers	Livestock	Mesa	Gold
Basin	Mining (-ed)	Lark Bunting	Louisiana Purchase	Border (-ed)

Colorado Bingo

Columbine	Plateau	Great Plains	Denver	Border (-ed)
Canyon	Executive Branch	Lake(s)	Livestock	National Park(s)
Blue Spruce	Crop(s)		Highest	Aquamarine
Pikes Peak	Stegosaurus	Rhodochrosite	Mesa	Rivers
Rocky Mountain(s)	Louisiana Purchase	Mining (-ed)	Ski (-ing)	Gold

Colorado Bingo

Judicial Branch	Bighorn Sheep	Lake(s)	Denver	Pikes Peak
Blue Spruce	Gold	Boulder	Continental Divide	Motto
Climate	Lark Bunting		Plateau	Painted Turtle
Livestock	Colorado Territory	Rivers	Georgetown Loop Railroad	Louisiana Purchase
Highest	Mining (-ed)	Border (-ed)	Centennial State	Mesa

Colorado
Bingo

Colorado Bingo

Colorado War	Four Corners	Gold	Basin	Colorado River
National Park(s)	Great Plains	Song(s)	Continental Divide	Aurora
Canyon	County (-ies)		Motto	Crop(s)
Rivers	Georgetown Loop Railroad	Mesa	Aquamarine	Lake(s)
Mining (-ed)	Centennial State	Plateau	Climate	Louisiana Purchase

Colorado Bingo

Boulder	Plateau	Colorado Territory	Basin	Border (-ed)
Bighorn Sheep	Columbine	Lark Bunting	Judicial Branch	Aquamarine
Four Corners	Colorado River		Rhodochrosite	Motto
Climate	Mining (-ed)	Rivers	Centennial State	Mesa
Pikes Peak	Stegosaurus	Louisiana Purchase	Livestock	Gold

Colorado Bingo: Card No. 23

Colorado Bingo

Boulder	Louisiana Purchase	Columbine	Plateau	Continental Divide
Gold	Border (-ed)	Lake(s)	National Park(s)	Motto
Crop(s)	Colorado War		Colorado River	Climate
Pikes Peak	Rhodochrosite	Rivers	Centennial State	Blue Spruce
Rocky Mountain(s)	Highest	Mining (-ed)	Great Plains	Stegosaurus

Colorado Bingo

Highest	Lake(s)	Plateau	Painted Turtle	Gold
Aquamarine	Blue Spruce	Judicial Branch	Boulder	Aurora
Georgetown Loop Railroad	Continental Divide		Rhodochrosite	Rivers
Song(s)	Pikes Peak	Stegosaurus	Mining (-ed)	County (-ies)
Border (-ed)	Columbine	Canyon	Colorado Hairstreak	Rocky Mountain(s)

Colorado Bingo: Card No. 25

Colorado Bingo

Gold	Plateau	Four Corners	National Park(s)	Colorado War
Livestock	Great Plains	Continental Divide	Columbine	Boulder
Georgetown Loop Railroad	Rhodochrosite		County (-ies)	Highest
Centennial State	Basin	Pikes Peak	Mining (-ed)	Rivers
Crop(s)	Colorado Hairstreak	Painted Turtle	Stegosaurus	Rocky Mountain(s)

Colorado Bingo

Four Corners	Canyon	Plateau	Columbine	Executive Branch
Pikes Peak	Rhodochrosite	Judicial Branch	Rivers	Aurora
Wings Over the Rockies	Stegosaurus		Mining (-ed)	Highest
Colorado War	Bighorn Sheep	Lake(s)	Rocky Mountain(s)	Aquamarine
Colorado Hairstreak	County (-ies)	Gold	Song(s)	Crop(s)

Colorado Bingo

Four Corners	Columbine	Song(s)	Plateau	Boulder
Executive Branch	Gold	Rhodochrosite	National Park(s)	County (-ies)
Stegosaurus	Climate		Crop(s)	Livestock
Ski (-ing)	Colorado War	Lark Bunting	Mining (-ed)	Rivers
Basin	Flag	Colorado Hairstreak	Rocky Mountain(s)	Pikes Peak

Colorado Bingo

Gold	Columbine	Colorado War	Judicial Branch	Flag
Mesa	Livestock	Lake(s)	Crop(s)	Song(s)
Georgetown Loop Railroad	Rhodochrosite		Aurora	Plateau
Executive Branch	Pikes Peak	Grand Junction	Mining (-ed)	Rivers
Boulder	Continental Divide	Rocky Mountain(s)	Bighorn Sheep	Stegosaurus

Colorado Bingo: Card No. 29

Colorado Bingo

Coloradan(s)	Plateau	National Park(s)	Flag	Rivers
Aquamarine	Columbine	Four Corners	County (-ies)	Aurora
Georgetown Loop Railroad	Colorado River		Crop(s)	Lake(s)
Rocky Mountain(s)	Bighorn Sheep	Basin	Mining (-ed)	Rhodochrosite
Pikes Peak	Tiger Salamander	Stegosaurus	Gold	Song(s)

Colorado Bingo: Card No. 30

www.ingramcontent.com/pod-product-compliance
Lightning Source LLC
LaVergne TN
LVHW061337060426
835511LV00014B/1968